To my real
Liza,

12 - 2 9 - 2020

Twilight
to
Son Shine

I have enjoyed our
friendship + hope to meet
you one day.

For information address:

J2B Publishing LLC
4251 Columbia Park Road
Pomfret, MD 20675
www.J2BLLC.com
GladToDoIt@gmail.com

Printed and bound in the United States of America.

This book is set in Garamond. Designed by Mary Barrows.

ISBN: 978-1-941927-81-6 - Paperback
          978-1-941927-82-3 - Hardback

Thoughts into Poetry
~ The 1st Poems ~

Twilight
to
Son Shine

Poetry and Photographs by Jim "The Houseboat Poet" McDonald
J2B Publishing

Dedication

I dedicate this book of poetry and all the good that might come from it, to my mom, Grace McDonald. Even though I initiated most of my problems in my life, she stood by me through them all.

Table of Contents:

Acknowledgements

I would like to thank my sister, Debbie McDonald, my friend, Matt Jones Jr., and friend and publisher, Jim Brewster, who all encouraged and pushed me to follow my dream of writing. Especially my old, really old and decrepit, one-hundred and ninety-nine-year-old friend, Raymond Davis, who kept saying, "Just do it!"

I would also like to express my gratitude for the expert tutelage received from Professor Krista Keyes at the College of Southern Maryland, La Plata campus.

Introduction

I've wanted to write stories and poetry for decades. When I became a disabled/retired carpenter I had time to devote to this passion; But would I?

Then a question I read online challenged me with, "If you knew no one was going to read your work, would you still write it?" Thought about the question for days, then I realized, "Of course I would!"

With *Twilight to Son Shine*, I begin the early release program for all the stories and poems incarcerated in my one celled brain. They need their freedom and to breathe the outside air.

mom

never called her mommy
never called her mother
never called her Grace
just mom

she cleaned my hurts
with iodine and tissue
dressed with Band-Aids
covered with love

loved me with smiles
loved me with hugs
loved me with food
loved me with spankings

my best chauffeur
my best teacher
my best friend
my best person

never stole from her
never yelled at her
never hurt her
so I thought

I never understood
till I was dad
all the work
she loved me with

dad

he was much taller
towering over me
closely behind him
in his foot steps

taught me to work hard
eat good and play right
closely behind him
in his foot steps

learned how to drive
at a young age
closely behind him
in his foot steps

learned how to drink
drank like a funnel
closely behind him
in his foot steps

walked in the garden
slue footed was he
closely behind him
in his foot steps

stepped in his foot prints
slue footed was me
closely behind him
in his foot steps

drank himself to death
my brother soon followed
closely behind him
in his foot steps

he never stopped drinking
I drank to follow
closely behind him
in his foot steps

my sons started drinking
just like me
closely behind me
in my foot steps

had to stop the bleeding
drinking I quit
a brand-new start
in my own foot steps

she left us

a month has gone by
she's still gone away
not a trace nor a lie
it hurts less everyday

no call text or knock
not a sound she gave
she left us in shock
when she went away

empty souls at nightfall
left us three all alone
tears seep before they fall
abandoned to the bone

that was then
forty years ago
no answers again
we still don't know

I'm gone

thought you knew
my love was true
I suffered no clue
you laid with a few

you blamed the drug
or maybe the jug
you implied "bah humbug"
then hide it with a hug

her ample beauty is thin
it ceased below the skin
that's where her ego begins
I'll never trust her agin

you done me wrong
for much to long
so bang the gong
because I'm gone

she said no

a sad response
it's hard to feel
a cheerful joy
would be ideal

but no such action
remains in sight
for the sinking ship
sank tonight

the blues

if I wrote music
it'd be the blues
paid by some
saddening dues

I want to create
a blues melody
but people would ask
what's wrong with me

depression

I sit
I lay
I stare
I stand

but don't relax
but don't rest
but don't focus
but don't test

I whisper
I scream
I touch
I weep

but don't speak
but don't voice
but don't feel
but don't cry

I breath
I creep
I peek
I hide

but don't exhale
but don't reveal
but don't uncover
but don't conceal

you notice
you question
you worry
you forget

but can't grasp
but can't know
but can't relate
But I can't

it just is

it's not your fault
it's not my fault
it just is

the hole in
the wall

the hole in the wall
controls my all

an anxious captive
peeking out
screen or glass
buffers the fright
how do I leave
how do I stay

the hole in the wall
controls my all

breathing is rapid
breathing is brutal
afraid to leave
afraid to stay

the whole in the wall
controls my all

afraid to live
afraid to die

the whole in the wall
controls my all

can't sleep

laid down to sleep a while ago
wasn't sleepy I was hungry
wondered what can I eat
thought about the frig
no food just water
steak no too heavy
hooters hot wings
yes spicy chicken
yes spicy women
yes skimpy clothes
plumb tuckered out
just thinking about it
COPD now I can't breathe
tired exhausted totally rung out
now I can roll over and fall asleep

cut my hair

was long and thin
with a bald spot
showed some skin
where hair was not

years of growing
with just one cut
wavy and flowing
added some strut

no money it cost
to let it grow
friends I lost
they didn't know

people were rude
said cut your hair
they were skewed
I really didn't care

grayish and white
not red anymore
it shined in the light
as it fell to the floor

when it was long
forever to clean
now that it's gone
shiny and sheen

Mack in
the hat

do not like
my silly hat

called Mack in
my silly hat

cheaply bought
my silly hat

green and white is
my silly hat

Mack in the hat with
my silly hat

tall and awkward is
my silly hat

little too tight is
my silly hat

did not want
my silly hat

gave it away
my silly hat

time

can't hear it
can't see it
can't feel it
or can I

elusive but
          all around us
forgotten but
          mirror finds it
lost but
          always here

can hear it
          slipping away
can see it
          fading away
can feel it
          wasting away
here it comes
          now

now

not yesterday
not tomorrow
only now

there's only this time
not another day
not another hour
not another moment
only now

what happened
no today
no hour
no moment
no now

this time is missing
in yesterday
in tomorrow
this time is lost
no now

my view

your wrinkles are deeper
crepe skin on your arms
you stretch and ache
no pills ever work
your eyes of pain
or is that wisdom
mixture of both
are you content
friendly while out
looking so happy
tucked in at home
you're sullen and blue
it's not a glass on the wall
that's my view in the mirror

life counting

birthdays

at fifteen
can't wait to grow up
you'll be the boss

at twenty
one more year is heaven
then you'll be legal

at twenty-five
your experience grows
but only you know

at thirty-five
you have your own family
this explains your parents

at forty-five
eyes and hair are going
but nowhere you want to go

at fifty-five
memory is vague and elusive
lost just like your keys

at sixty-five
you wonder why
you wanted to be older

at seventy-five
your favorite place
is your quiet chair

at eighty-five
you wonder how
you made it this far

a life well

spent

they are yellow orange and red
then die brown cut loose and fall
they're left grounded on their bed
these now dead leaves are so small

their vestige now part of the spread
the whole of all beings somberly die
there is no petty when we are dead
thus all flesh or flora must soon lie

thou soul of life lies ahead
this money and anger isn't true
thoughtful works should stay instead
treasured memories should be left to brew

I missed it

I missed writing poetry
short stories I do like
but a lyrical sound
structured verses
just feels right
rhyming words
are special to me
seven more poems
is a chapbook you'll see

déjà vu

the caller ID
screamed out her name
I shivered with joy
did she feel the same

he's hurt she said
her brother she meant
please come and help
my fears won't relent

I rushed to her aid
not knowing the plight
she pointed that way
too familiar the sight

he sat without motion
his name was Mike
he'll never smile again
he was ghostlike

I thought I'd be brave
I saw pale as a bone
I stepped to his form
I reached for my phone

a twenty-five in his ear
a really good friend
a little blood this time
not like my kin

déjà vu I did feel
now it's another
mom called before
when it was my brother

surprised I was not
their pains were many
physically they hurt
and fervor was plenty

each trembled with shock
as they pointed the way
neither could murmur
nor could they say

call turned from pleasure
to pain and despair
I remember them now
as a nightmare

counting
daisies

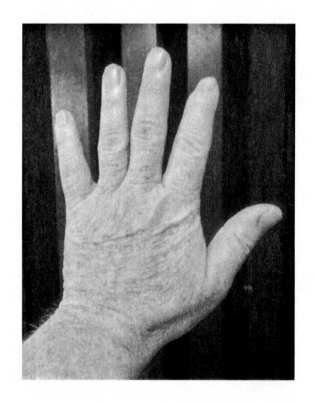

counting daisies
in a field of daisies

is like counting
blades of grass
in a square yard

is like counting
midnight stars
with no clouds

is like counting
white cars
in a metropolis

but not like counting
friends on one hand
among your acquaintances

friendship

February's surprise
was a beautiful day
much too nice
not to come out and play

met with some friends
wearing good clothes
fun was cut short
now going to Lowe's

meant to have fun
didn't expect chores
not in good health
to work on some doors

my back was just fine
till it twisted around
needed a few days
so I can rebound

shortness of breath
and an old bent spine
are two familiar failings
that keeps me off-line

two or three days
I'm down and out
but the same friends
always help me out

God's piece
of paper

found a sheet of paper
blank with not a mark
a white sheet of paper
pencil added some dark

yellow red and orange
the Son's perfect sky
watching over our space
then He added a butterfly

between water and grass
a little piece of land
not dark not light
that color's tan

the grass is bright green
the water invitingly blue
the old weathered pier
it's a beautiful view

the white sheet of paper
the colors gave it life
paints a peaceful picture
with not a line of strife

it comes in
threes

first give thanks
for all I possess
all You gave me
it could be less

then You gave me
Your only Son
He lives in my heart
which means I've won

next we start over
not necessarily new
but one more year
before we're through

the last five weeks
embraced all three
thanks birth new year
Your gifts to me

we're all invited in

knows what you've done
and where you've been
He quietly tells us all
we're all invited in

He loves everyone
regardless of our sin
catches us when we fall
because we're all invited in

faith says I've only begun
so, don't play the violin
trust Him till He calls
we're all invited in

God's slack to none
He forgives us within
2nd Peter 3:9 covers all
because we're all invited in

everlasting

dug deep in my heart
to cleanse my soul
can You forgive me
make me whole

You took my shell
a piece of coal
scrubbed it clean
and filled my hole

You saved my life
and rocked my roll
I'm forever pardoned
You paid my toll

Meet the Author

Jim "The Houseboat Poet" McDonald has been a Southern Maryland resident since 1965. In 1989, he turned towards Jesus and away from the drinking and drugs that had characterized his life for seventeen years. He lives on his houseboat, floating up and down with the tide, writing about life from the waterline. He is finally fulfilling a life-long dream of becoming a poet and writer.